Myrtle

Also from the Emma Press:

The Emma Press Anthology of Mildly Erotic Verse
A Poetic Primer for Love and Seduction: Naso was my Tutor
The Emma Press Anthology of Motherhood
The Emma Press Anthology of Fatherhood
Homesickness and Exile
Best Friends Forever (Dec 2014)
The Emma Press Anthology of Dance (Apr 2015)

The Emma Press Picks:

The Flower and the Plough, by Rachel Piercey
The Emmores, by Richard O'Brien
The Held and the Lost, by Kristen Roberts
Captain Love and the Five Joaquins, by John Clegg

Pamphlets:

Ikhda, by Ikhda, by Ikhda Ayuning Maharsi
Raspberries for the Ferry, byAndrew Wynn Owen
The Dead Snail Diaries, by Jamie McGarry
Rivers Wanted, by Rachel Piercey
Oils, by Stephen Sexton
If I Lay on my Back I Saw Nothing but Naked Women,
    by Jacqueline Saphra

Myrtle

By Ruth Wiggins

With an introduction by
Deryn Rees-Jones

for Saradha
with love from
Ruth
x x

THE EMMA PRESS

for Russell, without whom
no songs

THE EMMA PRESS

First published in Great Britain in 2014
by the Emma Press Ltd

Poems copyright © Ruth Wiggins 2014
Introduction copyright © Deryn Rees-Jones 2014

ISBN 978-1-910139-05-9

A CIP catalogue record of this book
is available from the British Library.

Printed and bound in Great Britain
by Letterworks Ltd, Reading.

theemmapress.com
editor@theemmapress.com

Introduction

To read a Ruth Wiggins poem is to take a side-step into
another world. That poetic world is characterised by risk,
energy, desire, delight in otherness and the dappledness of lan-
guage; it is a world in which, since I first began to read Ruth's
work a few years ago, I have taken a huge pleasure. There is
nothing predictable or safe about where these poems end up,
nor indeed about the journey on which they take you. Words
'glee-bounce' about and, as she also writes, get 'festive/ in the
wreckage of bonfires'. But this is not idiosyncrasy for its own
sake. People talk about the importance for a poet in finding
a voice. The reality is that we have many voices, and what the
poet must do at the start of a career is to find the most open
and deep version of the self he or she can find; or, as the poet
Anne Stevenson writes, to find a place where we can best
'inhabit poetry'. Ruth writes here with poise and humour,
underscored by a great certainty in language's capacity to hurl
us into new experiences and to transform our knowledge of
the world; and perhaps in her many conversations with the
old gods, her writing also comes from a sense that as human
beings there will always be dangers at our elbow. Elegant,
unafraid, and full of the joys and pains of being alive, these
poems say in the face of both ordinary and extraordinary
dangers, *Trust me*, and we are right to do so. We are right, too,
to answer the call they make when they make us laugh, or think
again, and also say to us as readers, '*Dare you*'.

Deryn Rees-Jones
September 2014

Contents

Against Perspective

At this vantage I am
m   a   s   s   i   v   e
here
I-can-bury-my-face-in-the-hillside
work the green with my fists
like a suckling cat
guzzle up   g   r   o   u   n   d   w   a   t   e   r
draughts of sap

I've Been Crumbling Anti-Histamines Into Your Food All Week

The brick belly of the house is fat with
She wants flowers? Well, let's see.

*

Blindfold off.

She pushes the bowing front door into *that's odd*,
push again, into the soft geometry of a corridor
of cherry. Traps of blossom spool across her feet,
the stairwell of their two-up-two-down newly solid
with three dimensions of pink.

Their living room bounces with rose attar, Fantin Latour.
Progress through to the kitchen heavenly, but slow.
Picked out in damask, bourbon and moss, the ghosts
of their fathers deal card tricks, argue the toss,
on the old sofa they'd dragged here

from who knows where. Nearly killed them; maybe did,
how hard they collapsed into it. How the neighbours
lined the street as lorry after lorry delivered its load.
His mother busy with a Thermos of tea; men wrestling
with tarpaulin. One tarp, bolshie

with sycamore, lurched across the street, each seed
pirouette twisting with other ideas; nearly took two men
with it. Upstairs, on a bed of promises and catkin,
he shows her his blueprint for an annexe of ragwort
and whitebeam. Sketches a cellar,

to be carpeted and lit: wellies, footballs, all newly minted
in the modest glow-worm light of lily of the valley.
He places several handheld, battery-powered fans, to stir
their bower of dandelion seed. Spheres bouncing
off eyelids, noses, toes.

The kids windmilling in, to spectacular effect. The small
miracle of not a single sneeze. By evening, each of their
waist-height boys is an anther. His ribs, hers, strip-lights
of gold. Bathing, a nonsense. Their one-in, one-out,
one-in of a bathroom, now green

with water hawthorn, miniature bogbean. Great-crested
newts run between the taps, making virtues of crumbling
washers: drip-drip darting, drip-drip splash. Outside,
the whole thing seeds itself up the street. Early outbreaks
of lovage, sweet briar, vetch.

Borrowed Time

This morning we mostly lay on the couch,
impersonating cats, talking gibberish.
This afternoon you fucked me, right out
of my pyjamas and into yours. This evening
we made a day of it, me in your vest,
you in nothing but the heat. We discussed
our old fan as it scythed the humidity;
considered the crooked blinds, how they
redrafted light into sheet music on the ceiling.
Then tonight, you slipped from my arms
into a sleep I could not share. Diving
without warning, you pulled the oxygen
tanks in after you. Leaving me trying
without hope to pick you out in the deep.

Adjustment

Come the apocalypse
and days of cellars
filled with the very
worst kinds of meat,
you and I, with our scant
supply of practical skills,

will have to rely on these
healing hands of yours.
Oh I know you're bored but
place them again over my
aching spine, feel the discs
shift and realign.

There will be gifts
and furs in tribute, of this
I'm sure. And probably
usurping girls to boot,
who I suppose I'll just
have to learn to kill.

Only The Lover

(after Propertius)

Silly mortals, always second-guessing
the hour of your death. Wondering
from which vantage point the ambush will spring.
Fortified with quantum woo,
raw milk, qabalah, mistletoe,
you send scouts to reconnoitre.
Decode communiqués of dice and bones.
Apply pi to the howling of dogs,
fuzzy logic to a FTSE in freefall.
You type your vital stats into deathclock.com
but from the Circle Line to Tora Bora,
all exit points remain hidden.
The whole thing's a cluster-fuck
with you dejected in the middle.
If not improvised explosives
with your name on,
it's the FUBAR of friendly fire.
What's more, when you get some R&R
your mind just runs and runs –
a home in flames, or levelled by tornadoes.
That oddball, stockpiling anthrax in his lock-up.
Truth is, only the lover
knows when he is done for.
And a lover doesn't waste nights,
restless over skies scudded
with missiles or freak weather.
For even if he was at death's door, stiff
in his Austin Reed, wedged
in a box stuffed with dismal silk,
if he so much as heard his sweetheart moan,
felt her breath upon him,
she'd find there was life in the old dog yet.

On Fear Of Your Flying

Staring at the puzzle of my belly in the bath,
I mutter dangerous prayers.

Hope that last embrace has left a trace –
your precious cells inside, kept safe.

Waiting charmed, on my command
to divide, and in division, conquer the divide.

Of course, I'll somehow know before I'm told
but imagine anyhow just how I will be told.

Whether it be your sister at my door, breaking
words like *fuselage, tundra, fall.*

Or your father weeping silently down the phone,
your mother in the background saying

you're making it worse, give me the phone.
Rehearse just which of these will be the one –

the precise moment when, knocked
sideways for breath and ready for spells,

I place a palm to my belly, kick-start
your clutch of cells – feel them startle

into memento mori, keepsakes,
poppets, a widow's company.

Reynard

Big old dog fox,
heavy with health,
with cock.
        The balls on you!
Curled up there, brassy in the sun.

I'd like to take hold of your snout,
feel the squeak
      of your teeth
against my thumb.
            Borrow your coat awhile,
     big old dog fox.

How long do you suppose before I'd turn?

Take to dossing on compost,
            hoodwinking crows.
     Stinky, hungry
for what it is that makes you blush.
Your cunning about my shoulders,
      quick words
rising in my throat.

           How long before I'd take
a foot to the itch behind my ribs?
Forget this knife,
     this aubergine dish.

Modern Herbal

Rosemary – sweet diminutive of Christmas,
the pine tree. And so much more *available*.
No wrestling with a six-footer in fishnets,
just pop some in your shopper. Alone in June
and out of season, throw some in a copper-
bottomed pan. Admire the rude, sapling bounce
as it hits the heat. No slew of other necessary
ingredients – simply infuse. Singe its small
branches, gloriously empty as they are of gifts.
Aromatic needles in a hot butter fizz; a festive,
baubled skid. Likewise, a smoking sprig
can be used as a smudging stick – rub some
between your fingers as you walk your perimeter;
deck your halls against unwanted guests.

Pulmón de manzana

November… December
months in the dark
puts her stethoscope tight
to the city's back
pressing here, then here
left a little, listening
sees if she can't tickle it into a cough.
February… March
casts an arm out the window, tests the air
flips a mirror to the city to see if it's still breathing
Bloomsbury fogging the glass
in plumes of Yes! still breathing
her image glee-bouncing
knock-down ginger round the block
giggling.
Months in the dark
behind blackout blinds and bolted door
beef and rice for breakfast
and beef
and rice
for breakfast
flowering in the dark in a cerise satin slip
thick fifths of bitter in her gusto-fisted grip
singing.
Filling out her Titian dumpling elbows
with bananas and molasses
spring cracking a courtyard laugh
that billows and bounces
off the north then south
east west walls of the whole city block
vaulting the cherry tree tops, now just pinking
pinking
her own private spinney into
hell yeah, still breathing.

Fourteen

Was it our six-month anniversary or seventh?
At this distance I forget.

Either way I do recall First Love's persuasive gifts.

He opened with the classic, two bottles
of Pernod, but from Paris came the clincher –
a small green hippo.

Enamoured with emerald glass,
I taught my tongue to love that vicious syrup,
toughened myself out of affectation –
anise, my new best poison.

At home, the hippo would snort and fart,
nose me clear of doe-eyed infatuation.
His bristly puss thick with green kisses, bellowing –
He's no good. Leave him.

Each afternoon he'd hoot and carp
over my diary's airtight encryption –
You know he's faithless. Don't you?

Let's head for the Zambezi, he roared
and cantered. *Although your mouth is small,
your teeth, frankly, feeble,
I'll teach you how to put the wind up
the white-water rafters.*

A decent offer.
But then, which right-minded teenager
wouldn't think so?

Last time we saw F.L.
he was all over the park on vodka schnapps,
in his pocket a small white tiger.

Birch

Prostrate birch –
what's with all the reaching?

So keen for something
that you can't get straight.

You lean. Invite me to
saddle up. Strong-backed

you speak to me
in mushroom and lichen.

Go on,
green my tongue.

Venus At The Potter's Wheel

Screw your Judaeo-Christian god –
his reputedly deft fingers,
opposable thumbs.

I could just as easily throw pots
with my thighs, shape your keen red clay
into an urgent vase.

Finish you off with a flourish
of myrtle – oh then you'd know
the meaning of fucked.

Demoiselles

Three schoolgirls hover
in a complex huddle of cigarette and gesture, casually batting away
a thin bouquet of smoke.

You look across to see
what has them so transfixed – the most earnest boy in the school
is engaged in a re-enactment.

He towers absurd
in segmented armour. An improvised lance and fluttering cape.
There's something

about the languor
of his enlisted princess – tied, bored and tokenistic, to an old football pole.
Something, moreover

about the weak movement
in the bin liners and tyre rubber, buckled into a simulacrum on the grass.
The flit of girls, the playing field,

all hold their breath,
at a loss for words, or any other means to record a small dragon
bullied to the ground.

False Widow

(Steatoda nobilis)

I sit at my desk bagging up
goldfish, while she folds
those grim silk weeds into
her false-bottomed drawer.

She's all carnival misdirection.
There! on a high wire.
Now! back in her booth.
Such a messy eater –

all narrow gut, no jaws.
It's a sideshow I can't bear
yet watch in awe. Rust-
flecked stains in her beard,

on my work, the walls.
She laughs when I juggle
dustpan and brush,
grins – *Hey clown shoes!*

What do you take me for?
I up the ante, look instead
for a more effective implement.
Take this twist of wire,

wound at the tip with
inches of bristle, it could
do the trick. Oh two can
play at this game, I think.

While she's off picking
fights with the marks and
starlings, I twist my stick.
Twist some more,

give it a bit of wrist.
Her grey candy web clings
and twirls. Such resistance,
it grumbles with delicious

static. What on earth
does she spin this wretched
stuff from? I pull hard,
mouth pursed, hope

she won't be on the end
of it: the whole bristle-mat
helter-skelter of her
skitter down the wall.

The Truly Beautiful

Sleeve-deep in stitch work, red-gold charcoaled in her hair,
she is a bird snared with lime, the perfect sitter. Footsure

on the boarding ladder, she is your Iseult, just a few short
hours before the seasick draught will bind her to another.

Not yet the yellow gorse, ghosting on a receding coast.
Not yet the strawberries, your wife fed by another's hand,

and publicly. Curse the kindness of the rocks that jut, yet
will not wreck the faint lines of the boat. Hold her course,

draw her to you. Oh love's burden, watch her turn
from you. But love can deny nothing to love. And already

the lady is in waiting, her hand at the crystal stopper,
the philtre. *I cannot paint her,* you say, *but love her.*

The Annunciation Of The Bean

There's a bonny lass on the garden step,
cross-legged, half-wishing that a broken wing
will pitch a swallow into her lap to heal.

And determined girls in a Petri dish
are busy, exponential, doubling down,
putting everything they've got on red.

And inside each peanut, as each child knows,
there's a patient goldfish about to flip.

And in a flat over Tesco, there's a pot of myrtle
from which, night after night, love creeps.

And a childless couple at the edge of town
watch eggshell seedlings on the windowsill.

And Thumbelina dances, one suitor to the next.
From Toad, to Cockchafer, to velvet Mole.
By minnow, by lily-craft, by song.

And violet petals fall from a walnut crib,
from which the miraculous girl has already flown.

From the golden girl in the sack of corn,
to the inch-high moon in the glittering bamboo,
love is the hunger that leaps the gap,

that licks the grate; the twist of wheat.
The stranger's pledge, give me coin or cow
for this here bean, this barleycorn, a prayer –

however small, let me be with child,
be she nothing but a sweet green sprig.

Leda

And did she imagine him later
in a coffin of rye paste sealed
with butter? Or picture herself
green and blistered, her furious
knit-one-purl throughout the night,
casting off a shirt of nettle leaf
come morning, her bitter jerkin
prickling his neck? Would she choose
to leave one sleeve undone, binding
him with knots, never more to ravish?
Five fingertips, ever-dipped now
in feathers. And all rewritten, whole
cosmologies of gods and rapists,
eagles, husbands, goats and showers.

Crawk

She's the opposite of mirrors,
a counterpoint to light.
Forces open the sky – any vista.
A reminder of what waits behind.
She puts paid to doubt
with her scrubbed-step economy.
Gathers subtlety up,
straightens him out.
Doesn't blink
at the designs of her deputies.
Knows each has an eye
on the carrion crown.
She plays pick-up-sticks
with her quarrel of sisters.
Drops in on aunts who teach her,
again, how to knit.
Keeps adding branches,
adding branches – coils of wire,
cobweb to her nest.
She skims black vowels across the sky.
Prefers the glitter
of earthworms to trinkets,
gutter water to fizz.
Puts her pipes to misuse,
barks and coughs.
Grouts her gizzard, gargles with rocks.
She gets festive
in the wreckage of bonfires,
warms her wishbone with embers,
grants no wishes.

On Making Love To A Nanny Goat

(Herculaneum, AD 79)

No need to rush or mount a rearguard action,
you've already won her over.

Goatherd, you've got her
eating out of your palm,

bleating at your jocund lays,
your charming way with Syrinx's bones.

So take this last paramour
face to face.

Ease her into your crib of reed,
bring her dainty hooves up to your chest.

Say what the hey if she should choose
to nibble at your coronet of pine,

so long as you bed your thyrsus
good, and deep, inside.

Her pleat is as soft
as the mountain hare skins

in which you were wrapped at birth.
Your back, exquisite, it falls

with grace, into the fleece
that curls about your arse and thighs.

Remember to take her gently
by the beard. Steady her as she goes.

No need to heed your hounds
giving tongue to some trouble

brewing in the hills. For now,
the wild mountain echoes

with well-hung chimes.
You yourself are heavy with bells.

Myrtus

(after Horace)

Gorgeous boy, there is no need to overdress.
I can't urge you enough – ditch the artifice.
There's no need to bring me pricey black roses.
        Thorny, unscented.

And you can lose that spider-spun suit as well.
Come to me naked – a simple myrtle sprig
bright between your teeth. Be mine, right here beneath
        this cheerful old vine.

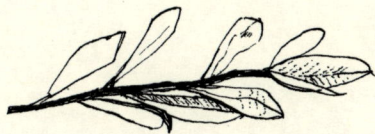

Notes

'Only the Lover': see Propertius *Elegy* II, xxvii.

'Pulmón de manzana': 'lung of the block', a green space at the heart of a city.

'Demoiselles': see Burne-Jones's *St. George & the Dragon* and Picasso's *Les Demoiselles d'Avignon*.

'False Widow': *Steatoda nobilis* is a non-indigenous spider; a messy housekeeper, it is often touted as Britain's Most Dangerous.

'The Truly Beautiful': see William Morris's sketch of his wife Jane in medieval dress, also his painting of her as *La Belle Iseult*.

'Leda': a mash-up of Leda and the Swan with the fairy tale, The Six Swans.

'On Making Love to a Nanny Goat': see sculpture of Pan, found in the ruins of Herculaneum.

'Myrtus': see Horace *Ode* I, xxxviii.

Acknowledgements

Thanks are due to the editors of the publications in which some of these poems first appeared: *Smiths Knoll; The Anthology of Mildly Erotic Poetry; A Poetic Primer for Love and Seduction; Peloton – Templar;* and *Bestiary – Poetry on the Lake.* Thanks also to the William Morris Gallery for displaying 'The Truly Beautiful' alongside Morris's drawing of his wife Jane.

'I've been crumbling anti-histamines...' was commended in the 2013 Battered Moons competition; and 'Adjustment' was commended in the 2011 Stanza Poetry competition.

My grateful thanks to everyone at Tideway and Forest Poets, particularly and with much affection: Anna Johnson, Nigel Pollitt, Jenni Hall, Rachel Smith and Susie Campbell. Thanks also to Jane Robinson, Jane Draycott, David Morley, and Alice Oswald. And lastly, a huge thank-you to Anja Konig, Emma Wright, Rachel Piercey, Deryn Rees-Jones, and the ever lovely Caroline Vacara.

About the poet

Ruth Wiggins lives in East London with her partner and their three sons. She studied English and Latin at Durham University. Her work has appeared in UK magazines and anthologies, and has been commended by Alice Oswald and David Morley in recent competitions. She enjoys photography; and a book of her photographs of women dressed as super heroes, *Wonder Women of America,* was published in 2008. She is a member of Tideway and Forest Poets. She also likes to hike.

THE EMMA PRESS

small press, big dreams

The Emma Press is an independent publisher dedicated to producing beautiful, thought-provoking books. It was founded in 2012 in Winnersh, UK, by Emma Wright and in 2014 the Press was shortlisted for the Michael Marks Award for poetry pamphlet publishers.

Our current publishing programme features a mixture of themed poetry anthologies and single-author poetry and prose pamphlets, with an ongoing engagement with the works of the Roman poet Ovid. We publish books which excite us, and we are often on the lookout for new writing.

Visit our website and sign up to the Emma Press newsletter to hear about all our upcoming calls for submissions as well as our events and publications. You can purchase our books and stationery in our online shop.

http://theemmapress.com

Also from the Emma Press

RASPBERRIES FOR THE FERRY, *by Andrew Wynn Owen*

ISBN: 978 0 9574596 5 6 – PRICE: £6.50 / $12

Andrew Wynn Owen dazzles in his debut pamphlet, whisking the reader up with his infectious rhythms and lively sensuality.

IKHDA, BY IKHDA, *by Ikhda Ayuning Maharsi*

ISBN: 978 0 9574596 6 3 – PRICE: £6.50 / $12

Reading this book is like being splashed with freezing water and showered with popping candy and wild roses.

OILS, *by Stephen Sexton*

ISBN: 978 1 910139 03 5 – PRICE: £6.50 / $12

Belfast poet Stephen Sexton evokes melancholy and a strange kind of romance throughout his brilliant debut pamphlet.

RIVERS WANTED, *by Rachel Piercey*

ISBN: 978 1 910139 04 2 – PRICE: £6.50 / $12

Rachel Piercey charms and disturbs in this beautiful, frequently heart-breaking collection of poems about love, identity and home.

IF I LAY ON MY BACK I SAW NOTHING BUT NAKED WOMEN, *by Jacqueline Saphra, illustrated by Mark Andrew Webber*

ISBN: 978 1 910139 06 6 – PRICE: £12.50 / $21

Saphra constructs an eerie, sensuous world with her wry descriptions of eccentric parents and step-parents.
